"Rob Pasick has a gift for touching the hearts of pet owners. He also knows that in most every dog there's a heart waiting to connect with a human being. You'll like Rob. And you'll like his dog Lucy."

— JEFF ZASLOW —
Columnist, *Chicago Sun Times*

ᘓ • ᘔ

"All who love dogs will love these lyrical observations by Robert Pasick."

— ERNIE HARWELL —
Hall of Fame baseball broadcaster

ᘓ • ᘔ

"Anyone who has loved a pet will find a soul mate in Robert Pasick. . . . A real heartwarmer."

— SHERYL JAMES —
Journalist, *Detroit Free Press*

ᘓ • ᘔ

"A warm, soulful collection of poetry . . . [that] will make you nod, laugh, and reflect on life and death. The last poem may make you cry."

— ANNE VALENTINE MARTINO —
Columnist, *The Ann Arbor News*

CONVERSATIONS
WITH MY OLD DOG

CONVERSATIONS WITH MY OLD DOG

For Anyone Who Has Ever
Loved and Lost a Pet

ROBERT PASICK, PH.D.

◼ HAZELDEN®

INFORMATION & EDUCATIONAL SERVICES

BOOKPLACE

Transitions to a New Life and a New World . . .

Hazelden, the leading recovery publisher in the world, has teamed up with Transitions Bookplace to create Hazelden Transitions, an exciting, new publishing imprint that explores the world of health and transformation for individuals, communities, and the planet.

www.hazelden.org

Copyright © 2000 by Robert Pasick

ISBN 1-56838-574-9

Cover design by David Spohn
Cover illustration by Susan Holdaway Heys
Interior design by Terri Kinne

EDITOR'S NOTE:
Trademarked names are used only in an editorial fashion
and to the benefit of the trademark owner with no
intention of infringement of the trademark.

This book is dedicated to Al and Lucy.

ACKNOWLEDGMENTS

Thanks to Chris Wozniak, Sue Holdaway Heys, Mary Cronin, Chris Galvin, and to my late, great friend Glenn Davis, who believed all along.

As always, deep appreciation to Patricia, Daniel, and Adam.

Dear Reader,

Do you ever talk to your dogs? I confess. I do.

When Lucy, our Yellow Lab and my first dog, turned thirteen in 1998, she still maintained her sweet disposition, but we could definitely see her growing old before our eyes. She could no longer hear well, had lost one eye to glaucoma, and hated to go out in the snow because she could no longer bear much weight on her rear legs. Despite her ailments, our whole family loved her more than ever and ached with the fearful anticipation that we might soon lose her.

As an only child, I had always longed for a dog, but until we brought Lucy home from the breeder's one night, I had never had one of my own. My mother had a fear of dogs, at least until Lucy worked her magic charms on her. Somehow, Lucy taught my mother to overcome her fear. Dogs do that for us. They help us to face the most difficult of emotions. My mother eventually learned to love Lucy as much as we do.

By age thirteen, Lucy had witnessed many changes in our family. When we first brought her home, our youngest son, Dan, was just entering kindergarten; now he is a college student. Adam was nine and had just started to venture out into the wider world; now he is a Web writer, living in New York City. I know Lucy noticed these changes, but she somehow managed to adapt.

At that time, my life was changing too. My wife, Pat, had begun a job that would require extensive travel. My dad had been forced to retire at age seventy-eight and was himself slowing down. My friend Glenn—a young fifty-five—had recently been diagnosed with lung cancer. And me . . . I was fifty, and my body reminded me of it daily.

When the boys left home that year after Christmas vacation, they feared they would never see Lucy again. Before they left, each spent tearful moments alone with her. They were saying good-bye before the fact, trying to imagine what life would be like without her. They had yet to lose anyone close to them, and Lucy gave them a chance to try on death, to anticipate their grief, and to guide them into adulthood.

Lucy had served as a spirit guide for me too. She was the canine muse for this book. For several months, every morning as I awoke early attempting to write, Lucy lay peacefully by my side, inspiring me to think and feel deeply. In talking to her, I was able to express myself.

On Lucy's thirteenth birthday, I thought about all the meaningful conversations we'd had, not just the normal master-dog, command-response exchanges, but soulful explorations—sometimes in my study but also while we were alone on a trail at County Farm Park. Talking to a dog can be like praying to an unknown God, to someone who understands but does not need to respond directly. With her expressive Lab face, her head cocked to one side, and those amber, imploring eyes, Lucy had always been an excellent listener. She rarely interrupted or turned the conversation to herself.

This book is a collection of my conversational poems to Lucy. If you ever talk to your pet, contemplate what it means to grow old, wonder about the origins of the universe, grieve losses, celebrate the miracle of a comet at sunset, give your dog ice cream, long for reunions with old friends, or talk to God or any Higher Power, this book may bring you some pleasure.

— Robert Pasick, Ph.D.

What Breed is God?

If God is a dog, what breed would He be?
    A Jack Russell Terrier—
        small, yippy, and fierce?
    Or a Labrador Retriever, with patience like Job:
        compact, strong, majestic, able to retrieve
            the most troubled of souls?

As a kid, I had two images of GOD-AS-DOG:
    The German Shepherd, Rin Tin Tin—brave, powerful
        and independent.
    The other (my secret hope), a Collie, like Lassie
        or better yet, the Martlock's dog, Laddie who was
            gentle, nurturing,
            with hair so abundant you could use her
            as a blanket
                or a pillow.

One-Pointed Attention

Lucy, I envy your one-pointed attention.
Never seeming to do two things at once,
     how do you get everything done?

I learned long ago to do several things at once.
My parents taught me through example:
     Dad could
          sit at the dinner table,
          eat,
          read the newspaper, always the funnies first, and
          carry on a conversation all at the same time.
     Mom always listened to the radio and glanced at
     the mirror, no matter what else she was doing.

I can't help but
     read while I eat,
     read while I use the bathroom,
     listen to the radio while I drive (and drink coffee),
     glance at the newspaper when I talk to someone,
     drink coffee as I do therapy.

Do you get distracted, too, Lucy?
     Do you fantasize about your pal Remington while
          playing ball?
     Do you dream of bones lost and balls found while
          you hold a sit-stay?

Do dogs worry about
        death,
        vision loss,
        hearing loss,
        incontinence,
        cancer,
        poverty?

Who is going to take care of you in old age?
        Will you experience doctor-assisted suicide without
                even asking for it?
        Where are you going when you die?

Or are you always here in the present,
        alert to the opportunity for
                food,
                the chance to go for a walk,
                for someone to pet you?

Teach me one-pointed attention, Lucy;
        I long to be here fully, too.

For me, being fully present is tough;
I may be in one place, but my mind is often somewhere else—
        in the future,
        in the past,
        in daydreams—just not here.

Lab Pup

Spending time with a young Lab yesterday,
    I was reminded how frisky you were in your youth:
        constantly on the roam,
        searching for something to chew,
        something to eat,
        someone to romp with.

Now, you still love to play,
    but you've grown serene.
        You want to be close to us.
        You want to be comfortable.
        You rejoice as people enter the house.

But you rest most of the time.

Lucy, have you discovered your Buddha nature?
Have you found enlightenment?

Even with one eye,
you see so deeply.

Trust and Fear

We walk in a new park.
A little child spots you.
Jumping with excitement, and knowing no fear,
  she approaches.

You two, the same height,
  greet each other with kisses.
Instinctively trusting you,
  she kisses your head.
You lick her face.

Moments later on a bridge, we pass another child.
  She rushes past you in terror,
    so afraid, she presses herself against the railing
    as you pass.

Why are some children so in love with animals,
  while others are locked in terror?

Your size terrorizes some, Lu.
Little do they know how gentle you really are.

Oh, what a joy it would be to teach a child
  to be free from fear of dogs.

Boys and Dogs

Lucy, today while thinking of you as a puppy,
 I remember Daniel as a little boy
  waking on a Sunday morning,
  dragging himself into the living room,
  clutching his blanket,
  and curling up next to me on the couch,
   he'd ask me to read him the Sunday funnies.

I remembered how his grandparents would love it when he
 joined them in their warm bed on a weekend visit.
 Maybe someday we too will have grandchildren
  join us in bed.

The need for cuddly babies is so strong.
We need to snuggle you dogs, too,
 but while dog lips turn me off,
 nothing is sweeter than a baby's kiss.

Yet you take care of us and we take care of you, too.
 We need each other—always will.

I guess our boys will always need us, too,
 but in different ways.

They go off to chase their dreams.
You go off to chase birds.

No, I am not inviting you to crawl into our bed
 in the morning.

Jack Russell Terror

You used to roll on your back to let us rub your tummy.
Since Ruby arrived, you avoid this trusting position.
    She, the tiny yet fierce Jack Russell,
        has frightened you.
    Maybe she attacked you when you were most vulnerable.

People seek therapy for such traumas:
    They have been hurt when vulnerable,
        hit by a parent whom they trusted,
            betrayed by a lover to whom they gave all,
           abandoned,
             deceived,
               tricked,
                  abused.
    They no longer can trust themselves or others.

Lu, I will work on teaching you to roll over again.

I will protect you from little Ruby
    who only tries to protect her tiny self.

We will work together.

Certainly you can help me daily with my own traumas,

For this I am eternally grateful.

Hearing Loss

Did you ever notice, Sweet Lu, how we can see lightning flash
     with our eyes still closed?

How sometimes we hear no thunder after the lightning?

Oh, I'm sorry, Lu,
     I forgot that you might not be able to hear the thunder
          at all—
     the vet told us you're losing your hearing.

To be deaf, such a loss in May.
     No morning doves singing.
     No frogs croaking.
     No gentle rain falling.

Knowing you, Lu, maybe you've discovered new sounds.

Can you now hear trees bud?
Grass grow?

Perhaps you hear the
heartbeat of God.

Is This Not Happiness?*

Is this not happiness?
>The sun sets as Lucy sleeps by my side.

Is this not happiness?
>I crave a sweet and find one helping of Ben & Jerry's
>>buried behind a bag of frozen soup vegetables.

Is this not happiness?
>A moment of peace with my Labrador Retriever
>>as I await my family to return home
>>to eat the meal I have prepared.

Based on a Chinese poem, author unknown.

Webs of DNA

Lu, today, I am in Spain with our boy, Adam.
    who thrives in this ancient culture.

Seville is a city of beauty and frivolity.
    Catholicism pervades—the images of the virgin are
    everywhere:
        on doors,
        on walls,
        in fountains,
        on altars.

You'd love it;
    . dogs roam loose and shit wherever they want.
    The sun shines daily;
        you would find many spots to catch warm rays.

I enjoy being with Adam,
    but I know you miss him.

Do you have images of him in your mind,
    or do you only think of him when he returns home
    and you smell him?

When do you first pick up his scent?
    When he drives down the block?
        Or maybe earlier, when he arrives at the airport?
        Or is it that last moment when he is about to
            open the garage door?

With children, we never need reminders;
 their presence with us always,
  our DNA connected to theirs with an invisible
  thread only a parent can sense—
   around the corner,
   down the block,
   across the Great Lakes and oceans.

   Woven through time and space by love.

Forgiveness

Lucy, you are honest and true.

You never resort to substances to cope with the exigencies
 of life.
>   Nor do you swear,
>   attack,
>   watch porn flicks,
>   cheat,
>   lie.

Sure, you steal a bit of food when no one is looking.
You may not be perfect, but you are an inspiration to those of
us who seek relief from
>   cheap thrills,
>   deceits,
>   and manipulations.

Nor are you self-righteous—a particularly unpardonable sin.

And you are so forgiving.
Oh to be able to forgive and forget like a dog.

Maybe Jesus,
>   who was said to forgive someone seventy times seven,
>   studied your species for his inspiration.

Bittersweet Victory

Lucy, do you miss your father?
Michael certainly does.

After the Championship victory, Michael raced to get the ball,
    clutched it to his chest,
    and fell to the ground
        crying.

Others jumped on top,
    but he was alone in his tears.

When the teammates got off, he ran to the locker room,
    still squeezing the ball.

He crawled under a wooden bench,
    as if the sobs would bring life back to his dead father.

He dedicated the game to him;
    fatherhood was his greatest accomplishment.

In his most courageous victory he grieved
    publically,
    emotionally,
    for his greatest loss.
        Opening his heart for
            every man who has lost a father,
            for every father who has abandoned a child.

Lucy, I bet your father grieved in his own dog way.

Mystery Toenails

We danced around your toes this morning, didn't we, Lu?

We did our old familiar "Rob trying to clip Lucy's nails" dance.
I brought along Fig Newtons to reward you for
cooperative behavior,
but you scarfed them down when I wasn't looking.
Cookies consumed.

Then, as I grabbed a paw, you kept backing up.
Finally, with some smooth talking,
you relaxed enough to let the clipping begin.

I snipped the first nail on the left paw without incident,
but when I reached for the right,
I discovered those nails looked like they had already
been clipped.

Funny, I couldn't remember clipping them,
and no one else in the family cuts your nails.

So I have a mystery:

Did I clip your nails but forgot,
did someone else clip them,
or have they stopped growing?
That possibility intrigues me, scares me.
What would that mean?

I remember my grandma dying.

The doctors said as long as her nails continued to grow, she
was OK.

She would not die.

Yet she did.

The Vet

Sorry,
I tricked you yesterday.

You hobbled into the car expecting the park.
Instead, I drove you to the vet's office
    to have your diseased eye removed.

So difficult to explain the concept:
    "This may hurt, but it's for your own good."

We also fear the difficult path,
    confronting the tough issues.

I do this for a living.
I encourage people to make the toughest choices:
    and yet in my own life I, too, hesitate,
    dreading pain as much as the next guy.

I'm going to pray for your speedy recovery
    so that once again you can have fun
      —like removing an old sandwich from Dan's backpack
    and eating it on your pillow
    when no one is looking.

No Prozac for You

Lucy, you hang your head whenever you've done wrong.
Yet, you rebound from your guilt
    with our first friendly gesture.
A "good girl" is all you need to revive your spirit.

No Prozac for you, Lu.
After a few minutes with your head buried in your pillow,
    you're like a new dog,
        ready to roll over and play once again.

Self-Acceptance

Spring has returned,
    but the spring in your step has not.

You rise slowly;
    jumping into the car
    is now an effort.

That's OK,
    I will lift you,
    I will go at your pace.

Easier to accept a dog where she is
    than a person,
        whom we push and cajole
        to do more or change.

Easier to accept you where you are
    than to accept myself?

Losing Things

Do you ever lose things?

I've seen you hunt for a tennis ball,
>
> but you do not obsess.
> You give up and go to your pillow.

Not I.

I've spent a total of 14 years,
>
> three months,
> three days,
> and three hours so far
> searching for lost stuff.

How could I be so dumb as to have misplaced that
>
> check, wallet, watch, glasses, keys, phone slip, notebook,
> tape, ring, knife, toy, blanket, glove, sock, medicine bottle,
> paper, book, hat…

My idea of heaven is a pile of my lost stuff
>
> —a lot of good it will do me there.

Better to think I'll ultimately find all the answers
>
> to my most perplexing questions

> —like how much do dogs know?

Super Senses

You sniff danger, Lu,
>responding to smells I do not even know exist.

You smell warnings born on airwaves
>I have no access to.

You are ever aware, ever scanning,
>even as you sleep.

You sense ice falling before it clings to the branches.

I wish you could teach me, Lu, how to master the super senses—
>to be able to intuit like you do.

Do I, too, possess these powers, but fail to activate them?

I am your willing student.
Teach me in these last days of winter.

Worry

You watch us prepare for a trip.
>You look forlorn.
>Do you wonder whether we'll take you with us?
>Do you fear you'll be left alone?

I often wonder,
>do dogs worry?

I've spent half my life fretting about what may never come
>—accidents, illnesses, financial setbacks, abandonments,
>failures of spirit, failures of courage, humiliations.

I like to believe you don't worry, Lucy.

You're of peaceful mind.
>But I am not sure.
>You can look so sad sometimes,
>>so fearful.

Maybe God designed special worries for each species
>that reflect those of His own.

Jill

How do you handle the awful pain of grief?

Our wonderful friend Jill is gone.
As I look down upon you at my feet, I fear, next you?

She has left the world a far better place; she has brought cheer
and hope to all who knew her—canine and human alike

Let's pray to all the gods we know, Lu, to take care of her soul
and to enjoy her company.

The dogs in Heaven are in for a treat.

A Trained Mind

Lu, do you believe a trained mind brings health and happiness?
If so, how do you train your mind?
> While you appear to be sleeping are you secretly
> meditating?
> Are you talking to God on the sly?

Some say dogs sit closer to God than does man.
> Dogs don't kill each other,
>> don't quest after material gain,
>> and get over their quarrels quickly.

You appear balanced and serene.
You live a life mystics only seek.

Teach me, Lucy, to be my compass
> on the road to enlightenment.

Control

We make a bed for you outside our room;
> yet, in the morning we find you
> asleep on the couch,
>> the same one we have tried in vain
>> for 13 years
>> to keep you off.

You are a rare blend:
> a loyal dog with a mind of her own.

We can no more control you
> than you control our new puppy, Ruby.

We people spend much of our time on the illusion of control—
> we order our lives and try
>> to order the lives of others.

However, we learn—as with you—
> that we may get folks to sit
>> but never to stay.

Anger

Do you understand my anger?

As much as I love you, you have made me angrier
      than anything or anyone in the past 13 years…

      peeing on the porch,
      eating our filet mignon,
      tracking mud,
      bleeding on the carpet,
      running off,
      jumping up on people,
      barking incessantly.

When I come home and you hide your head in your pillow,
      you look guilty,
      and I know you're avoiding my wrath.

Yet, my anger didn't stop you from jumping on the counter
      to eat a whole loaf of Zingerman's Farm bread!

Maybe I vent my anger on you
      instead of dumping on the kids.
Maybe I just do the proverbial kick the dog routine.

Getting angry at a dog
      is about as useful as anger at the weather.

Don't Leave Yet

You gave us a real scare, Lu,
> You go to the vet for a rabies shot,
>> collapse,
>> and your heart stops.

Frantic calls to experts at the vet school at Michigan State—
> we learn you were just so scared, your whole system
>> shut down.

You made us encounter the unthinkable—
> someday soon you will die.

I've never lost anyone close to me.
I don't know how I will take it.
I know I will miss you terribly.
I know Ruby will prove some consolation, but
> I will cry,
> I will hurt…

I can think of no profound ending for this poem,
> except to say I love you.

(When I say those words to you, you don't seem too moved.)

(How about a cookie instead?)

> (Now we're talking!)

The Dog-O-Matic

A bright Sunday morning.
    You choose to lie in the light and clean yourself—
        legs, paws, anus—you are one clean dog.

But we plan to take you to the new Dog-O-Matic dog wash.
    Do they do cleaning inside and out,
        undercoat, miracle wax, toe-nail cut?

New experiences can be petrifying.
Last night at the hospital MRI lab,
    they spun my protons to the sounds of
        pneumatic drills and
        computer beeps.
They said, "Don't move for 35 minutes."
I repeated the prayer of St. Francis 30 times.

Was St. Francis of Assisi a forward thinker?
    Did he write the prayer with me in mind?
        Born in 1181,
        Francis Bernadone left home after a sudden illness
          at age 22
            to rebuild Christ's church.

Did he envision a 51-year-old Jew in 1998 America
    lying perfectly still in a metal cylinder
        while his protons were activated by magnetic
        compressors
        that took a picture of his discs—
          all the while reciting his prayer?

Imagine, Lu, 800 years from now in 2798,
    a guy on some asteroid reciting "Lucy, Lucy, my
    Sweet Lucy"
        over and over again,
            in that eternal effort to free himself from fear.

Maybe we'll just wash you in the tub.

Rejuvenated

Lu, you're miraculously rejuvenated.
    Science has pitched in with a new medication, Rymadol.
Suddenly, your hips ache no more;
    you bound up the stairs,
    chase squirrels,
    bring the ball to play fetch.

We live in an era of true medical miracles.
Soon they'll be replacing dog body parts.

Which one would you want replaced first?
    Your left eye, to be able to see fully again?
    Or, your ear, to hear the rustle of chocolate bars
        being unwrapped.

Fortunately, no need to replace your soul—
    still as sweet as ever.

Luckily, scientists haven't worked out that mystery, yet.

Planner

How do you get along without a planner?
In the entirety of your 13 years,
> I have never known you to have any sort of planner
> > or organizer.
> Yet, your life seems orderly and, as far as I can tell,
> > you rarely forget anything!

With me, it's a different story.
> I have organizers to organize my organizers.
> I have two Franklin Planners,
> three different sizes of pocket planners,
> electronic Palm Pilots,
> and an index card holder.
> I have an Ironman watch with an alarm,
> > a timer,
> > and a stop watch.
> I have notebooks,
> Post-It notes in three sizes,
> pens with three choices of ink (red, blue, and black),
> > and pencils.
> I have two computers: one standard and one portable.

This is not a lie, Lucy, I waste time each week just trying to
find my organizers!

Obviously I need your help.

> What is your secret?
>
> Please let me know before I have a nervous
>> breakdown precipitated by an acute case
>> of plannus overwhelmus.

When I die I fear St. Peter will ask me to recite the seven
habits of highly organized people,

> and I won't be able to find my Palm Pilot to look
> them up.

Play Ball!

What is this renewed interest of yours in playing ball?
    What a treat!
    After a long lull, you have revived our game of catch.

Like the old times,
    you lie down in the kitchen doorway, nose first.
    I roll the tennis ball, you block it with your nose, and
    you push it back to me along the wooden floor.

Rob playing catch with his dog, Lucy. So peaceful.

It reminds me of the games of catch I'd play with Dan and Adam.
    Dan, of course, never peaceful in sports.
        At age five, he'd rear back and throw the ball so hard
            I had to buy a catcher's mitt.
    Adam was never thrilled about baseball.
        For him, shooting hoops replaced catch.

I don't remember playing catch with my dad.
    He worked too many hours, and then was too tired.
    He'd try, but mostly I played catch with myself.

I'd toss the ball high on the side of our house,
    then leap against the Monroe's brick wall next door,
        trying to make a leaping catch like my heroes
        Al Kaline or Mickey Mantle.

I could entertain myself for hours waiting for the guys to come
    out to play.

First, touch football in the fall with Mike Martlock
    —four years older, tall, and very cool.

Always playing quarterback,
teaching us the drills he'd learned from Lefty Brandt
or Ted Meister, the Ferndale High football coaches.

Then, street hockey on the frozen street in the winter.
Mrs. Fernstein would yell at us every day as she'd run
over the bricks we used to mark the goal lines.

And of course, baseball in the spring and summer,
sometimes on the street,
often at Paul L. Best school on the corner.
More than anything I wanted to be a great baseball player.

Occasionally, we'd invent new games like
running bases,
or, later, we learned spin the bottle from Nancy Monroe
and her orphaned cousin Tina.
Much different than catching a towering fly ball
against her bedroom window,
yet equally as thrilling.

As we grew older, we played ice hockey on backyard rinks.
I remember getting drilled on the forehead by Mike's
slap shot.
Then I pulled myself up from the snow bank
—shock, but no blood.
And I made the save!

Or tackle football without pads.
Dale Mars and I got into a fist fight in the last game
I can remember.

So let's play on, Lucy.
Just bark when ready,
because I'm always up for a good game of catch.

Squirrel Killer

You were right about Ruby, Sweet Lu.

She is a tough little dog.

After years of chasing,
    she caught a squirrel,
    brought him to the steps of the porch
    —shaken dead.

Later, I went to get the shovel to bury him,
    but upon my return Ruby was out back,
        and I had to search for her conquest.

From the wood chips I could see a squirrel tail pointing skyward.
    Ruby had buried her prize squirrel,
        but couldn't get it deep enough
        to conceal the tail.

        Or did she want to display it like moose antlers?

I don't know about Ruby: squirrel killer, hunter, pet?

Maybe some day we'll teach her to fetch
    —like you, Sweet Lu.

Yoga Dog

Life seems to be ever more difficult for you.
Your back leg so weak, you fall down frequently.
>   We've taken to tying a yoga belt around your middle,
>   so we can boost you up the stairs.

Maybe we can enroll you in a yoga class.
>   Yoga for old dogs. Why not?

One of the basic yoga stretches is called the "Downward
>   Facing Dog."

Of course, we would never make you learn the "Cat Stretch."

The Privilege of Aging

The privileges of aging:
> You awake at 4:53 AM barking.
> I know immediately you need to go out, but I ask anyway
> > "What is it Lu?,"
> > hoping I've mis-heard the meaning of your bark.

You answer by heading to the door.
I raise myself, and then I let you out back.

A few minutes later,
> you bark again to come in from the rainy night.

I try to coax you up the porch steps.
> Again, no luck.

So I go out into the cold night,
> barefoot, in shorts, and a sleeveless shirt,
> > hoping no one is looking.

I grab your collar and up you go.
I do not pull,
> you just need my hand on your collar to provide
> reassurance
> > that you won't slip on the wet stairs.

When I am old,
    I will need a helping hand too.
    We all do.

If I were blind,
    you'd be my seeing-eye Lab.

As you age, Lucy, rest assured;
    I'll be your seeing-eye guy.

Lucy in the Snow

You're a 13-year-old dog,
    but you still love to roll on your back in the snow.

Don't you ever stop to think of your age?
    How many winters in the park?
        How many remain?
    What's appropriate for an old dog to do?
        What is not?

Do you associate a pain in the hip with old age,
    or does it just ache?

Do you envy the vigor of young pups and long for the restoration
    of your own energy?

Do you thrill at the moments of sudden found energy
    as you race for the Frisbee?

"Sure," you say, "I can't sustain it
    —for long—
    but it sure feels good as I bound across the snow to retrieve.
    I am damn proud of my retrieving powers.
    I will retrieve until I drop.

When I die, I'm going to retrieving heaven
    where masters throw balls all day,
    where Frisbees fly like birds,
    where patches of snow lie in summer meadows
        just to cool me down,
    where gravity is no obstacle in my capacity to leap.

Any Frisbee, as far as any master can throw
    I can catch.
        I am the Willie Mays of dogs."

You Take the Lead

What did you think of our walk at County Farm Park last night?
For the first time ever, I let you take the lead.
>I bet you were surprised when I took off your leash and
>followed you wherever you wanted to go.

At first you kept looking back,
>wondering what in the world I was doing.
>But after a few minutes,
>>you moved boldly ahead.

I must thank you.
You led me to places in our familiar park, where in 13 years
  of walking
>we've never been before.
>Like the public gardens,
>where people without their own property can use
>>16 square yards of earth to grow whatever
>>they want.
>What a delightful surprise—a horticultural mosaic of
>>flowers and vegetables of imaginative design,
>>>like a people's patchwork quilt springing to life
>>>>in the middle of the city.

I like going at your pace, Lu.
>Much slower than mine.
>Plenty of time to enjoy the dusk dance of the fireflies.

I watched you sip from the dew of tall grass,
>roll on your back on a patch of sage,
>sniff the universe on a fence pole.

From now on I will try to practice going away from the
  usual path,
        slowing down,
        taking my time,
        exploring,
        meandering,
        rolling on my back under the stars.

Instead of my habitual rushing.
I will try lollygagging through life,
Like the wise dogs do.

Winter Solstice

You probably wonder where all the sound has gone.
> Once again savage ear infections steal your capacity to
> hear the sweet sounds of life.
> You seem confused and scared; you bark frequently,
>> trying to hear some noise—even if it is your own.

On top of all that, you probably wonder where all the light
is going.

Let me assure you, you are not going blind; the light will
return.

Today is the shortest day of the year, but gradually the sun
will return to make the days longer.

Christmas is almost here.
> Just look outside.
> White lights have sprouted on trees and houses.
> Spirits are lifting.
> Hang in there.

Daniel and Adam will be home soon.
The house will be bursting with music, food, and laughter.

Old in the Winter

Tough January so far; snow so deep you have to poop near the
house, which you hate.

It's bitter cold, yet you can no longer make it through the night
without having to pee.

You love lying on the porch,
but after a few minutes on your belly,
the cold forces you in.

Roads so slippery your weak back leg slips and slides constantly.

No fun being old in the winter.
Even cheerful Lu gets grumpy.

Does your dog good sense tell you spring will soon arrive?

Do you wait for the Robin's song?
Sadly, some Robins, tricked by a warm November and
December never left.
We feed them, hoping they will survive.

We hope you'll survive another winter.
Even if we have to get up at 4 a.m. to let you out in 40°
below wind chills. No problem.

What we won't do for the dogs we love.

Friendship

Lucy, I want you to know I appreciate our long-term friendship.
We've sustained being buddies for 13 years.

But you're by no means my longest lasting friend.
> I keep my friends for a long time.

You've taught me so much about friendship.

> When you greet an old friend, they have no doubt about
> your love for them.

> And you never forget someone you've befriended.
>> Even if you've not sniffed someone for years,
>> you greet them with the same level of enthusiasm
>> as if you'd been on vacation together for weeks.

So let's celebrate our friendship.
> You are absolutely my best canine buddy.

Old Age Inactivity

Today I take my dad to the neurologist for yet another test.

I suspect he'll suggest my dad do some physical activity—
      he's become a couch potato.

Why do old people tend to become sluggish?

I see it in you, too, Lu.
      You sleep most of the day.
      I now have to coax or drag you
      for a walk to the park.

"Use it or lose it," they say.

      So keep going, Lucy.

      The longer you walk, the longer you will live.

Sensitivity

Last night's dog program on The Animal Channel gave me new
   respect for your dog powers:

> —a dog that ran into a mother's shower to warn her that
>   her five-month-old child had stopped breathing,
> —a dog that brought the phone to his master, who lay on
>   the floor having suffered a heart attack,
> —a dog so sensitive she can alert her diabetic master that
>   his blood sugar level is falling,
> —search dogs with such feeling that they grieve when
>   they discover no living survivors in an exploded building.
>   Their trainers have to play a game where they pretend
>   they have been rescued in order for the dog to feel OK.

All of this no surprise to me.

> You know when we're hurting.
> You know when we need comfort.

I cry and your head is in my lap.

If I ever sign up for sensitivity training,
I want you as my instructor.

Success Seductions

I keep getting off track, Lucy,
   seduced by success,
      craving for fame and fortune,
         yet really yearning for connection.

How difficult to find the true path;
   and once I have found it,
      to stay upon it.

Maybe I need your strong sense of smell Lucy.
   Once you get the scent, you keep going ahead.

Teach me to trust my nose;
   teach me to keep following my dream,
      the tear-sent scent of
         truth,
         conviction,
         passion,
            and bliss.

Holding Up

Now we resort to old-dog devices to keep you going.

> Non-slip booties for your weak back leg,
> An extra-short leash to guide you up stairs,
> A booster for your dog dish,
> Gravy on your food,
> We even tie a sling around your rear.

You keep hanging in there.

> You can hear a little,
> > especially hand claps.

> You push the ball a few minutes a day.

> You'll go for a walk with us, but only to the end of the
> > block.

Yet, you still bark at the paper boy, charge over to greet Sue
and Ron,

> and howl at the full moon.
> Not at all bad for an 85-year-old.
> You and my dad are now about the same age.

Last night he and I went to Bennigan's to watch the Super Bowl.

> For the first time, he ate nachos and shrimp fajitas
> > without guilt.
> I bought him a draft Molsons.

He's got his aids too: a hearing aid and a cane.

Like you, he retains his warm personality.

Luckily, while bodies deteriorate,
    sweet dispositions prevail.

Nine-Lives Syndrome

You, a dog, are beginning to show signs of the "nine-lives syndrome."

Last week we thought you were near the end.
>We even discussed how we would put you down,
>>whether we would bring Adam and Dan home
>>to see you.

Yet, with encouragement from our friend Mark,
>we stood by you,
>played with you more,
>took you out for a short walk.

The twinkle is back in your eye.

Last night, you pushed the ball down the steps 20 times.

You are a survivor, Lu. Just like my friend, Glenn.
>A year into his cancer, he suffers one set-back after
>another:
>>blood clots, fluid around the heart, swollen feet,
>>shortness of breath, a cough that will not cease.

Yet, almost every day, he works out at the gym,
>even if he only walks once around the track.

He sees patients every day, goes to his kid's performances
and games,
>and always asks how I am doing.

Sunday, for his 56th birthday, we are planning a big party for him.

> He's invited 40 friends he wants to thank for supporting him through his illness.

Thank us? We should thank him for being such an inspiration to us all.

You two are cut from the same cloth, Lu.

Till We Meet Again

Sadly, Lu, today I write to you in your sweet hereafter.
    I trust and pray that you had a safe and painless journey.

Lucy, you must have been surprised to have my dad join you
  so soon.
I bet he arrived with a lifetime supply of doggie cookies
    …he always loved dogs so much, yet, as far as I know,
      he never had one of his own.

As usual, Lucy, you were wiser than we could ever have imagined.
    Holding you as you died helped us prepare for
      Dad's passing, only one month later.

His body failed,
    but death itself was sudden.
    Pat and I sat with him as he died.
      Two days of struggle to leave his body,
      and then a peaceful final passing.

At the moment of his death, a single bird flew into our view.
    I pray that bird carried his soul to yours, Lu.

Now I pray Dad cares for you as his pet, and you watch over him
    wherever you may be.

I feel comforted imagining you two playing together, nurturing
  each other
    until, perhaps, some day
    we may all meet again.

WESB SITES DEALING WITH PET LOSS:

www.In-Memory_Of_Pets.com

www.Lightning-Strike.com

www.thepetchannel.com

www.amby.com

www.superdog.com

www.petloss.com

www.deltasociety.org

www.aplb.org

About the Author:

Robert Pasick, Ph.D., is a clinical and corporate psychologist at the Ann Arbor Center for the Family. He teaches in the Executive Education Program at the University of Michigan Business School. A popular keynote speaker, Rob has consulted to companies throughout the world. He is the author of three books about men: *Men In Therapy, Awakening from the Deep Sleep,* and *What Every Man Needs to Know.* This Is his first book about man's best friend. Rob and his wife, Pat, have two grown sons, Daniel and Adam, and a dog named Ruby, bless her soul.

Dr. Pasick is currently working on a book about the conversations other people have with their dogs. If you have any dog stories you'd like to share with the author, you can reach him at RPasick@aol.com or visit his website at www.Pasick.com.

Hazelden Transitions is an initiative between Hazelden Foundation's Information and Educational Services division and Transitions Bookplace, Inc.

Hazelden Information and Educational Services helps individuals, families, and communities prevent and/or recover from alcoholism, drug addiction, and other related diseases and conditions. We do this by partnering with authors and other experts to deliver information and educational products and services that customers use to aid their personal growth and change, leading along a wholistic pathway of hope, health, and abundant living. We are fortunate to be recognized by both professionals and consumers as the leading international center of resources in these areas.

Transitions Bookplace, Inc., founded in Chicago, Illinois, in 1989, has become the nation's leading independent bookseller dedicated to customers seeking personal growth and development. Customers can choose from more than thirty thousand books, videos, pamphlets, and musical selections. Authors appear frequently for special events or workshops in the Transitions Learning Center. Also available in the store is a legendary collection of exquisite international gifts celebrating body, mind, and spirit.

This Hazelden Transitions Bookplace initiative is dedicated to all brave souls who seek to change courses in their lives, their families, and their communities in order to achieve hope, health, and abundant living.

Transitions Bookplace
1000 West North Avenue
Chicago, IL 60622
312-951-READ
800-979-READ
www.transitionsbookplace.com

Hazelden Information and Educational Services
15251 Pleasant Valley Road
Center City, MN 55012-0176
800-328-9000
www.hazelden.org